This book is dedicated to my favorite people: Ian, Sydney, Luca, Kennedy, and Nathaniel.

Thank you to the following individuals for their support and editing during this project:
Melody Bergman, Jared Gillins, Tina Mattson-Bonett, Fiona Leikness, Zac Hourigan, and
the ladies of the Fair Oaks Ward (Gabby, Mary, Leslie, Holly, and Shelley).

If you enjoy this book, please consider leaving a positive review on Amazon.

For great resources and information, follow us:
Facebook: www.facebook.com/lds.eduempowerkids
Instagram: @empower_ldskids
Websites: www.empowerlatterdaysaintkids.org and www.educateempowerkids.org

The POWERS *of* HEAVEN:

A Priesthood Guide for Latter-day Saint Girls and Boys

By Dina Alexander, MS

Illustrated by Danelle Prestwich
Design by Jera Mehrdad

Introduction

We are living in a wondrous, yet sometimes turbulent time here on earth, and are thus facing many unique challenges. To empower ourselves and others, it is essential for us to understand our priesthood power and how it can strengthen and protect us, as well as increase our ability to receive personal revelation.

This book is meant to be read together—a child and parent or teacher learning together. Talk over the new and familiar concepts. If you are looking for a more meaningful experience, try an activity or discuss the questions in the workbook.

This book introduces some deep topics and reiterates some basic ones. Each page is full of significant information. Feel free to read and chat about just a few pages at a time, and if possible, read it together more than once.

"I will give unto the children of men line upon line, precept upon precept, here a little and there a little; and blessed are those who hearken unto my precepts, and lend an ear unto my counsel, for they shall learn wisdom; for unto him that receiveth I will give more."

—2 Nephi 28:30

Note: Not all of your questions about priesthood will be answered in this book. This is just the beginning. You must study this topic further and receive your own personal revelation. You can find more information on many of the principles discussed in this book in Section 3 of the General Handbook of The Church of Jesus Christ of Latter-day Saints.

*Important Words: Throughout the book, we have bolded certain terms that you can find in the glossary.

Long ago we lived with our Heavenly Parents.

They loved us dearly.

"There never was a God, and there never will be in all eternities, except they are made of these two component parts; a man and a woman; the male and the female."

—Erastus Snow

They nurtured and taught each one of us. They prepared us to come to Earth, to receive a body, to be tested, and to experience joy and sadness.

One by one, They gifted each of us—both girls and boys— with astonishing talents and abilities.

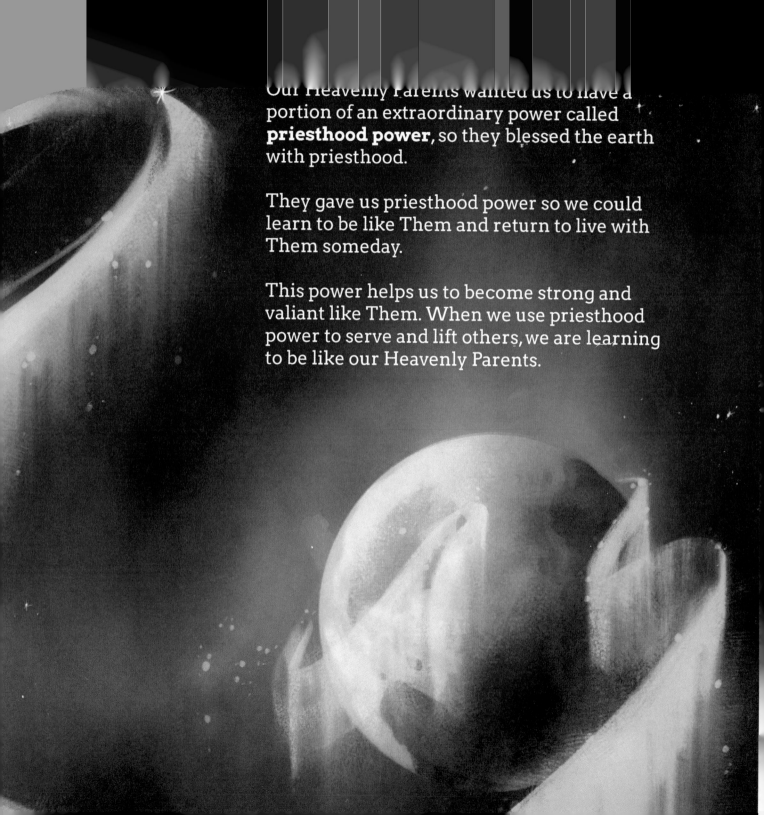

Our Heavenly Parents wanted us to have a portion of an extraordinary power called **priesthood power**, so they blessed the earth with priesthood.

They gave us priesthood power so we could learn to be like Them and return to live with Them someday.

This power helps us to become strong and valiant like Them. When we use priesthood power to serve and lift others, we are learning to be like our Heavenly Parents.

Our Heavenly Parents gave both men and women priesthood power.

They gave men and women different but equally important responsibilities here on Earth. Remember, "equal" does not mean "identical."

They appointed women to bear children and to nurture and help raise them. They appointed men to **administer** the priesthood and to also nurture and help raise children.

Motherhood and fatherhood are both vital parts of priesthood. Both men and women have power, and both have a responsibility to nurture and love others.

Although not everyone will have the opportunity to be married or have children in this life, both women and men have the same access to priesthood power and its blessings.

"And in his wisdom and mercy, our Father made men and women dependent on each other for the full flowering of their potential. Because their natures are somewhat different, they can complement each other; because they are in many ways alike, they can understand each other. Let neither envy the other for their differences; let both discern what is superficial and what is beautifully basic in those differences, and act accordingly."

—*Spencer W. Kimball*

Our Heavenly Parents love their sons and daughters perfectly. For this reason, They appointed both men and women to work together, to teach one another, and to serve others with kindness and compassion.

To better understand priesthood power and our ability to connect to it, there are some important principles we need to explore. Let's begin.

What Is Priesthood?

First, priesthood is the total power and **authority** of our Heavenly Parents. Using this power, God created and governs the heavens and the earth.

Second, in our Earth life, priesthood is the power and authority that God gives to men and women to act in *all things* necessary for the salvation of God's children.

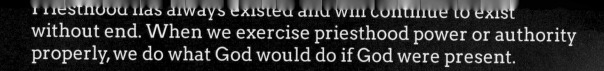

Priesthood has always existed and will continue to exist without end. When we exercise priesthood power or authority properly, we do what God would do if God were present.

Priesthood can be exercised in many ways. It is exercised when a woman **presides** over the Relief Society as the president. It is also applied when a stake President extends a call to the stake Young Women's presidency or when a father gives a blessing of healing to his wife or child. In the temple, priesthood is used when either men or women perform certain priesthood ordinances.

Covenants Give Us Priesthood Power

Every person who makes covenants with God and keeps those covenants has direct **access** to the power of God: priesthood power. All of us increase in priesthood power by making and keeping sacred covenants.

We make our first covenants in The Church of Jesus Christ of Latter-day Saints when we are baptized and confirmed as a member. When baptized, we make special covenants to keep the commandments and to always remember Jesus Christ. We also promise to stand as a witness of Christ.

As we keep these covenants, we can ask for strength and protection in our challenges, and revelation to guide our daily lives. We can even ask for angels, seen and unseen, to watch over us!

When you are older, you can access further priesthood power when you receive your **endowment** in the holy temple. An endowment is a gift of spiritual knowledge and power.

"Our Father in Heaven is generous with His power. All men and all women have access to this power for help in their lives. ALL who have made sacred covenants with the Lord and who honor those covenants are eligible to receive personal revelation, to be blessed by the ministering of angels, to commune with God, to receive the fullness of the gospel, and, ultimately, to become heirs alongside Jesus Christ of all our Father has."

—*M. Russell Ballard*

While receiving your endowment, you will make more covenants with God and receive great blessings and insight by keeping those covenants. It is important you return to the temple often. Spend time there and let God teach you.

Both women and men are endowed with the same power: priesthood power. Whether we are married or single, we all have full access to the priesthood power and blessings available to God's children.

You can prepare to make and keep sacred covenants by studying the scriptures and applying their teachings to your life. You can likewise seek personal revelation by praying often and sincerely.

You can attend your church meetings, ask questions, and partake of the sacrament. Seek to strengthen your testimony. Learn to minister to people in your family and community.

These are powerful ways to prepare to make covenants!

"If you are endowed but not currently married to a man who bears the priesthood and someone says to you, 'I'm sorry you don't have the priesthood in your home,' please understand that that statement is incorrect. You may not have a priesthood bearer in your home, but you have received and made sacred covenants with God in His temple. From those covenants flows an endowment of His priesthood power upon you."

—*Russell M. Nelson*

"Are you willing to pray to know how to pray for more power? The Lord will teach you . . . If we will humbly present ourselves before the Lord and ask Him to teach us, He will show us how to increase our access to His power."

—Russell M. Nelson

How Can I Connect to Priesthood Power?

"Righteousness is the qualifier for each of us to invite priesthood power into our lives."
—Linda K. Burton

We can access priesthood power when we pray from our hearts, sincerely and thoughtfully. We can also take time to study the scriptures and do family history.

Avoiding laziness and earnestly trying to keep our thoughts clean will further increase our priesthood power.

Fasting, being obedient to the commandments, and looking for ways to love and serve others can help us access priesthood power as well.

Read about spiritual gifts in Moroni 10:8-18 and seek to develop yours!

You can also ask for a priesthood blessing—requesting this power in your life.

What Can Block Our Ability to Exercise Priesthood Power?

Our ability to use our priesthood power can be closed off by focusing too much on the things of the world.

In order to access priesthood power, we need to get away from worldly activities and sins. Lying, stealing, gossiping, fighting, bullying others, using social media excessively, and viewing pornography will diminish our priesthood power.

God doesn't expect us to be perfect, but we are expected to try our best.

"Behold, there are many called, but few are chosen. And why are they not chosen? Because their hearts are set so much upon the things of this world, and aspire to the honors of men, that they do not learn this one lesson—that the rights of the priesthood are inseparably connected with the powers of heaven."

—Doctrine and Covenants 121:34-36

What are the Blessings of the Priesthood?

There are many great and marvelous blessings of the priesthood. These blessings are available to everyone who receives the gospel.

Because we have priesthood authority in The Church of Jesus Christ of Latter-day Saints, we have the amazing opportunity to be baptized and receive the gift and companionship of the Holy Ghost.

We can also take the sacrament and serve with priesthood authority in our callings and duties.

We can receive **patriarchal blessings** and blessings of healing or comfort too.

One of the most incredible blessings we can receive is the ministering of angels. This means as you make AND keep your covenants, you can have angels be near you, watch over you, and speak to you. Although most of us won't see these angels, we can feel their presence.

When you are endowed, you can also benefit from increased reason and understanding, as well as physical and spiritual protections.

You may also be sealed to your spouse for time and all eternity and can become joint heirs with our Heavenly Parents.

There are also countless blessings you can receive that are personal and known only to you!

"Priesthood power, much like the gift of the Holy Ghost, comes from our loving Father in Heaven and from our personal righteousness. In keeping our covenants with the Lord, we have the opportunity to receive revelation about ... everything for which we seek guidance. There is nothing that is important to us that is unimportant to the Lord."

—Jean B. Bingham

Priesthood Has Always Been on the Earth

Although **priesthood keys** have not always been on the earth, priesthood power has and will always be available on the earth.

Even during the Apostasy, before priesthood keys were given to Joseph Smith, righteous men and women all over the world worked through priesthood power to accomplish miraculous things.

*"All blessings come from God's total priesthood power and authority. **Priesthood power and blessings, by that expanded definition, have been and always will be available to all who qualify for them** . . . God's power was manifest at a time when conferred priesthood did not exist on the earth. Many spiritual and devoted individuals complied with laws that govern reception of God's blessings without having received any priesthood ordination."*

—*Dale G. Renlund and Ruth Lybbert Renlund*

Priesthood Keys and Authority Were Restored.

In 1829, while Joseph Smith and Oliver Cowdery worked to translate the Book of Mormon, they learned about baptism and a wondrous power and authority used among the Nephites. Wanting to learn more, they went into the nearby woods to pray about it.

As they prayed to find answers, John the Baptist appeared to them. He then put his hands upon their heads and ordained them to the **Aaronic Priesthood.**

Soon after John the Baptist's appearance, the ancient apostles Peter, James, and John also appeared to Joseph and Oliver. Under the direction of Jesus Christ, they **conferred** the **Melchizedek Priesthood** upon them.

*"How I yearn for you to understand that the restoration of the priesthood is just as relevant to you as a woman as it is to any man. Because the Melchizedek Priesthood has been restored, both covenant-keeping women and men have access to '***all*** the spiritual blessings of the church' or, we might say, to all the spiritual treasures the Lord has for His children."*

—Russell M. Nelson

What are Priesthood Keys, Priesthood Power, and Priesthood Authority?

Keys of the priesthood "unlock" the door to the power of God. The Lord confers keys when He gives permission for the use of His power.

When a person has priesthood keys, he has the right to direct the work of God in a certain area or over an organization. Keys also include authority over specific ordinances and activities such as baptisms, confirmations, and administering the sacrament.

A bishop holds certain priesthood keys for his ward so he can call and set apart ward members to various callings, authorize ordinances, and know how to bless those who live in the ward boundaries. A temple president holds priesthood keys to direct the work for the temple over which he presides.

Priesthood keys do not exist outside The Church of Jesus Christ of Latter-day Saints on Earth.

*You can find more information on priesthood keys in the workbook.

Priesthood Power and Priesthood Authority are Different from Priesthood Keys.

Both boys and girls have access to priesthood power. An eight-year-old girl or boy who has been baptized into The Church of Jesus Christ of Latter-day Saints can access priesthood power as they keep their baptismal covenants and live righteously.

Priesthood authority is the permission, given by someone who holds priesthood keys, to act in a calling or assignment.

Both women and men have this authority when **set apart** by a leader who holds the priesthood keys of presidency, like a bishop or mission president. Missionaries—both men and women who have been set apart—have priesthood authority when they teach a lesson to investigators or ask them if they would like to be baptized.

We need priesthood authority in order to perform ordinances like baptism, confirmation, and those done in the temple. In the temple, both men and women can not only exercise priesthood authority, but also administer ordinances.

*You can find more information on priesthood authority and priesthood power in the workbook.

"We are not accustomed to speaking of women having the authority of the priesthood in their Church callings, but what other authority can it be? . . . Whoever functions in an office or calling from one who holds priesthood keys, exercises priesthood authority in performing her or his assigned duties."

—Dallin H. Oaks

Priesthood at Home
and Priesthood in the Church

"Mine is a home where ev'ry hour is blessed by
The strength of priesthood pow'r,
*With **father and mother** leading the way"*
–Janice Kapp Perry, *Love is Spoken Here*

The priesthood functions differently in the family than it does
at Church.

At home, a mother and a father are equal partners, presiding over their
home together. Each has unique and special responsibilities.

In the Church we have a hierarchy and organization of priesthood keys
and authority so individual wards and the whole church run correctly.
This hierarchy is approved of by the Lord.

In our earth life, we have both systems of priesthood, but in the
eternities, we will have only the familial system of priesthood,
sometimes called patriarchal priesthood. This priesthood will have all
the keys, ordinances, and power needed for eternal life.

"In the eternities, it will be the fullness of the priesthood—the patriarchal or
familial system of the priesthood—that will continue . . . How different would it
be if we truly realized that the temporary hierarchical structure of the Church is
meant to support the familial/patriarchal structure of the eternal family?"

—Barbara Morgan Gardner

We Can Use Priesthood Power to Fulfill Our Missions Here on Earth

"I didn't realize, earlier in my life, that I had access, through my covenants, to the power of the priesthood. Sisters, I pray that we will recognize and cherish priesthood power as we 'cleave unto [our] covenants,' embrace the truths of the scriptures, and heed the words of our living prophets."

—Joy D. Jones

Our Heavenly Parents gave us priesthood power so we could fulfill our part in the Plan of Salvation. They intended both sisters and brothers of The Church of Jesus Christ of Latter-day Saints to receive ALL the gifts, blessings, and privileges of the priesthood.

Someday you may hold callings and be set apart by those who have priesthood keys. As you honorably work to fulfill your church callings and family duties and keep your covenants, you will be strengthened by priesthood power and have the opportunity to bless the lives of others with priesthood authority.

Both Boys and Girls are Essential in the Priesthood-directed Work of the Church

You don't need to wait to be an adult to discover and use priesthood power. As you keep your baptismal covenants, you can exercise your priesthood power right now.

God gave you specific missions to fulfill while on Earth. Take time to ponder the privilege that priesthood power is. Learn about spiritual gifts, pray, and ask many questions.

In doing this, you will discover what your divine missions are. You will come to understand your purpose for being here on Earth at this time and how to best use your priesthood power!

Remember, our Heavenly Parents blessed you with priesthood power and they trusted you to come to Earth at this important time.

You are stronger than you think,
loved by God more than you know,
and so much more divine than you imagine.

How will you use your priesthood power to bless and help others?

Family Workbook

"The Priesthood is everlasting—without beginning of days or end of years; without father, mother, etc. If there is no change of ordinances, there is no change of Priesthood. Wherever the ordinances of the Gospel are administered, there is the Priesthood."
—Joseph Smith

Use the following information and questions to inspire personal or family study about the priesthood of God.

You Can Learn About and Access Priesthood Power Now

God's holy priesthood, like other gospel topics, is deep and multilayered. It can be an enormous blessing in our lives if we are willing to receive it. Sometimes "receiving" it means putting time and energy into understanding and exercising this power in faith.

It's not enough to simply know that priesthood power exists. We need to study its parts, learn how to access it, and exercise it to bless our lives and those around us. There are several things we can do to better interpret this power and understand how we can exercise priesthood power. We can keep our baptismal covenants and obey God's commandments so we can keep the Holy Ghost's presence in our lives. Having the Holy Ghost reveal priesthood truths to us when we pray or study the scriptures is vital to gaining new understanding of the priesthood.

Questions to Consider:
- The prophet Joseph Smith used the words "everlasting," "eternal," and "eternity" to talk about the priesthood. What do these terms tell you about the nature and importance of the priesthood?
- Can you share a time when you were blessed by the priesthood?
- How can you prepare to receive the blessings of the priesthood?
- What covenants did you make at baptism? What can you do to keep those covenants so you may exercise priesthood power in your life?
- Why is partaking of the sacrament such an important priesthood blessing/ordinance?

We Need the Temple to Further Access Priesthood Power

"That thy servants may go forth from this house armed with thy power, and that thy name may be upon them, and thy glory be round about them, and thine angels have charge over them ."
—Doctrine and Covenants 109:22

When the time is right, we can be richly blessed by receiving our temple endowment, returning often, and spending time talking with God. In the temple we can be taught the mysteries of God and important truths for our personal lives.

It is essential to prepare yourself to enter the temple, receive the ordinances there, and make sacred covenants with God. The best way to prepare for entering the temple is by keeping your baptismal covenants, following the standards in *For the Strength of Youth*, learning to repent of your mistakes, and doing your best to live a virtuous life. Remember, you don't need to be perfect—you just need to do your best. Before you go to the temple, you'll have interviews with your bishop and stake president to help you be sure you've prepared yourself to go.

In the temple, men and women are endowed with knowledge, priesthood power, and authority. Even though a woman is not ordained to a priesthood office, she still receives priesthood authority and power through the ordinances of the temple and by keeping her covenants. Although only men are allowed to perform priesthood ordinances outside of the temple, both men and women are authorized to perform ordinances in the temple.

"Each ordinance gives additional power, blessings, understanding, intelligence, and light to each individual. Each draws us closer, as women and men, to becoming like our Heavenly Mother and Father."
—Barbara Morgan Gardner

After receiving your endowment, you may return to the temple as often as you wish to learn truth, meditate, and be close to God. Because the temple has been dedicated, it is a very sacred place. Like our homes, it is a wonderful place to pray for answers and ponder the mysteries of God. The blessings to be found in the temple are limitless.

One of the greatest blessings of having temples is that a man and a woman may be married and sealed together for time and all eternity. This unity between a husband and a wife makes exaltation possible. Julie Beck taught, "Neither the man nor the woman can ascend without the other. We are inseparably connected in that way."

"The Lord loves to do His own teaching in His holy house. Imagine how pleased He would be if you asked Him to teach you about priesthood keys, authority, and power as you experienced the ordinances of the Melchizedek Priesthood in the holy temple. Imagine the increase in priesthood power that could be yours."
—Russell M. Nelson

Questions to Consider:

- How can you prepare to enter the temple and receive your endowment, make sacred covenants, and receive those priesthood blessings?
- Why is receiving your endowment of knowledge and priesthood power in the temple so important?
- How can receiving your endowment help others?
- Why do the highest blessings of the priesthood (temple sealing) require both a woman and a man united in marriage?

Why Do We Need Priesthood Keys?

"With a set of keys, you can do a lot of things that you wouldn't otherwise be able to do— enter buildings, drive cars, and open trunks, among other things. Keys, basically, mean authority and access. The same is true of priesthood keys. They control access to the blessings and ordinances of the priesthood."

—The Church of Jesus Christ of Latter-day Saints

Priesthood keys are the authority and power to direct, organize, lead, and govern in the Church. The Lord authorizes the use of His power through priesthood keys. We need priesthood keys so things function correctly, as outlined by the Lord.

Priesthood keys are given by the laying on of hands when a priesthood holder is set apart to a presiding leadership position. Although women are set apart and exercise priesthood power and authority in their callings, they do not hold keys. God has never explained why women are not ordained to the priesthood, but we know God loves us perfectly and God's plan for us is perfect. The president of The Church of Jesus Christ of Latter-day Saints holds keys for the entire church, all over the world. But all keys have limits. For example, a bishop only has keys for his ward and a temple president only has keys for the temple where he presides. Once a person is released from a key-holding calling, he no longer holds keys for that geographical area or the people there.

Questions to Consider:

- What are the keys of the priesthood and who holds them?
- What are some examples of callings that require priesthood keys?
- Why do people in presiding leadership callings need priesthood keys?

Priesthood Authority

"In my callings, because I am serving with priesthood authority given to me by one who has keys, there have been numerous times when I have had thoughts or words given to me that are just what a young woman or Relief Society sister or Primary child needed to hear."

—Jean B. Bingham

Priesthood authority to serve in the Church is delegated to members by setting them apart to a Church calling or by assigning a certain job to them by their presiding Church leaders who hold keys. Like keys, priesthood authority also has limits. A stake Young Women president's stewardship includes authority over the leaders and young women living in her stake, but not any other stake. The same principle holds true for an Elders Quorum president or Sunday School teacher.

There is a difference between the authority of the priesthood and the power of the priesthood. Priesthood authority comes from ordination. Power comes from personal righteousness.

Questions to Consider:
- Who are some people that have priesthood authority?
- What does their authority allow them to do? How does it enable them to bless other people?
- Why are there limits to priesthood authority?

Priesthood Power

Priesthood power is the power by which God blesses His children. As we keep our covenants, we can receive personal revelation, promptings, and understanding that will guide us on how we can serve loved ones and those in our community. We can also receive much-needed strength to overcome difficulties in our lives and fulfill our missions here on Earth. Most importantly, we can draw upon priesthood power for the necessary courage and energy to be more like Jesus Christ and our Heavenly Parents.

Questions to Consider:
- Who can access priesthood power?
- What are some things you can do so you can access priesthood power?
- What are some "worldly pursuits" you can avoid in order to have access to priesthood power?
- If you felt you weren't worthy to call upon priesthood power, what could you do about it?

Activity:
Priesthood Requires Power

Whether you have been ordained to an office in the priesthood or not, you cannot have priesthood power without personal righteousness.

Show your children something (lamp, small appliance, toy, etc.) that is powered by electricity. Then show them it cannot work without the proper power. Explain how the object can be useful and a blessing to your life, but not without power.

Ask your child:
- What is making the object work?
- How is this like priesthood power?

Explain how priesthood power can provide light and blessings to those around you. Explain that a person may have been baptized, gone through the temple, and/or ordained to an office in the priesthood, but if they are not keeping their covenants and trying their best to be righteous, they will not have priesthood power. Together, read Doctrine and Covenants 121:34-46.

Ask your child:
- What can you do to be worthy of accessing priesthood power?
- Do you have to behave perfectly to have access to priesthood power? (No.)
- How can someone have priesthood authority but not priesthood power? (If a person is not living a righteous life, they will not be able to tap into this power.)
- What does it mean to "aspire to the honors of men" as stated in verse 35?
- How can we avoid setting our hearts "upon the things of the world" as mentioned in verse 35?
- How can we use our priesthood power with persuasion, gentleness, kindness, and pure knowledge as stated in verses 41-42?

Receiving the Priesthood as a Boy or Man

"In a coming day, only those men who have taken their priesthood seriously, by diligently seeking to be taught by the Lord Himself, will be able to bless, guide, protect, strengthen, and heal others. Only a man who has paid the price for priesthood power will be able to bring miracles to those he loves and keep his marriage and family safe, now and throughout eternity."

—Russell M. Nelson

Under the direction of those who hold priesthood keys, the Aaronic Priesthood and the Melchizedek Priesthood are conferred on worthy male Church members (Doctrine and Covenants 84:14-17). After the appropriate priesthood is conferred, the person is ordained to an office in that priesthood, such as deacon or elder. A priesthood holder exercises the priesthood according to the rights and duties of that office (Doctrine and Covenants 107:99).

Each man in The Church of Jesus Christ of Latter-day Saints should strive to be worthy to receive and use the Melchizedek Priesthood to serve others. When a man receives this priesthood, he makes a covenant to faithfully fulfill his priesthood responsibilities.

The Melchizedek Priesthood

The Melchizedek Priesthood is "the Holy Priesthood, after the Order of the Son of God" (Doctrine and Covenants 107:3). It is the power by which the sons and daughters of God can become like Him. This priesthood holds the key of the mysteries of the kingdom, the key of the knowledge of God, and the keys of all the spiritual blessings of the Church (Doctrine and Covenants 84:19).

Melchizedek Priesthood holders are promised to have "the privilege of receiving the mysteries of the kingdom of heaven, to have the heavens opened unto them, to commune with the general assembly and church of the Firstborn, and to enjoy the communion and presence of God the Father, and Jesus the mediator of the new covenant" (Doctrine and Covenants 107:19).

These massive blessings apply to all who make covenants in the temple—MEN AND WOMEN.

The ordained offices in the Melchizedek, or higher priesthood are:
elder, high priest, patriarch, seventy, and apostle.

"By intentionally making service to others part of our life, we will discover the mysteries of God. We will discover peace, find strength, and receive an increase of power as we serve our Savior, Jesus Christ, and strive to be His hands to lift and bless those around us."

—Bonnie H. Cordon

Questions to Consider:
- What is the real name of the Melchizedek Priesthood?
- What are some miracles Jesus performed using His priesthood?
- Is the priesthood Jesus Christ held different from the priesthood power men in the Church hold today?
- What must a man do to qualify to receive the Melchizedek Priesthood?
- What are some of the blessings we receive through those who hold the Melchizedek priesthood?

The Aaronic Priesthood

The Aaronic Priesthood is "an appendage to . . . the Melchizedek Priesthood" (Doctrine and Covenants 107:14). It empowers people to serve one another and prepares them to receive the blessings of the Melchizedek Priesthood.

The Aaronic Priesthood includes the keys of:
- The ministering of angels
- The gospel of repentance
- Administering in outward ordinances, including baptism for the remission of sins

The ordained offices in the Aaronic Priesthood are: deacon, teacher, priest, and bishop.*
*The bishop is the president of the Aaronic Priesthood in his ward.

Levitical Priesthood

The **Levitical Priesthood** is an order in, or a part of, the Aaronic Priesthood. Moses and Aaron belonged to the tribe of Levi. While the Levitical order does not function today, its privileges and authority are embraced within the Aaronic Priesthood for whatever future use the Lord may direct.

Questions to Consider:
- How does a young man receive the Aaronic Priesthood?
- What can a boy do to prepare to receive the Aaronic Priesthood?
- What responsibilities do deacons, teachers, and priests have?
- How does holding the Aaronic Priesthood prepare someone to receive the Melchizedek Priesthood?
- What does it mean that the Aaronic Priesthood holds "the keys of the ministering of angels, and of the gospel of repentance, and of baptism by immersion for the remission of sins"?
- What are some situations when you may feel the need to ask God to send angels to protect or guide you?

Activity: Memorize the Oath and Covenant of the Priesthood

(Doctrine and Covenants 84:33–39)

God has said those who receive the priesthood and obey the covenants that pertain to that priesthood will receive "all that [the] Father hath."

Make a personal goal to read and memorize the Oath and Covenant of the Priesthood:

"For whoso is faithful unto the obtaining these two priesthoods of which I have spoken, and the magnifying their calling, are sanctified by the Spirit unto the renewing of their bodies. They become the sons of Moses and of Aaron and the seed of Abraham, and the church and kingdom, and the elect of God.

And also all they who receive this priesthood receive me, saith the Lord;
For he that receiveth my servants receiveth me; And he that receiveth me receiveth my Father;
And he that receiveth my Father receiveth my Father's kingdom; therefore all that my
Father hath shall be given unto him.

And this is according to the oath and covenant which belongeth to the priesthood. Therefore, all those who receive the priesthood, receive this oath and covenant of my Father, which he cannot break, neither can it be moved."

Questions to Consider:

- How does this oath and covenant apply to both men and women? (It applies to everyone who makes covenants in the temple.)
- How do men "receive the priesthood"?
- How do women "receive the priesthood"?
- What does it mean when these scriptures say those who receive the priesthood and obey the covenants that pertain to that priesthood will receive "all that [the] Father hath"?
- What did Boyd K. Packer mean when he said, "There is an oath and covenant of the priesthood. The covenant rests with man; the oath with God"?

Priesthood in the Family:

"The gospel plan is implemented through earthly families, and our highest aspiration is to perpetuate those family relationships throughout eternity. The ultimate mission of our Savior's Church is to help us achieve exaltation in the celestial kingdom, and that can only be accomplished in a family relationship."

—Dallin H. Oaks

Familial priesthood, or **patriarchal priesthood**, functions quite differently than priesthood in the Church. In the home, a mother or matriarch acts in full partnership with a father, or patriarch of the family. They each have equally important responsibilities to look after their family and guide their children in a loving, righteous, Christ-centered way.

Activity: Father and Mother Leading the Way
Read or sing the words to "Love is Spoken Here" by Janice Kapp Perry.

I see my mother kneeling with our family each day.
I hear the words she whispers as she bows her head to pray.
Her plea to the Father quiets all my fears,
And I am thankful love is spoken here.

Mine is a home where ev'ry hour is blessed by the strength of priesthood pow'r,
With father and mother leading the way,
Teaching me how to trust and obey;
And the things they teach are crystal clear,
For love is spoken here.

I can often feel the Savior near
When love is spoken here.

Questions to Consider:

- Is priesthood power in our home *only* when Dad is there?
- Is priesthood power in our home *only* when Mom is there?
- How can each member of our family help our home be a place that is blessed every hour by priesthood power?
- How have your family members benefited from having priesthood power in your lives?
- Why does a difference in divine responsibilities between men and women make people think one is more important than another?

"Motherhood is not what was left over after our Father blessed His sons with the privilege of priesthood ordination. It was the most ennobling endowment He could give His daughters, a sacred trust that gave women the guiding role in partnering with our Father in the act of creation."

—Sheri Dew

Get to Know and Apply Priesthood Scriptures to Your Life

We can study prayerfully all the truths we can find about priesthood power. The following is a list of some very helpful scriptures to better understand priesthood power, keys, and authority. Get to know these scriptures and the general conference talks that discuss priesthood. As you do so, you will come to understand your opportunities to access priesthood power and help others.

- JST, Genesis 14: Melchizedek's ministry
- Hebrews 7: Information about the Melchizedek priesthood
- Moses 6:7: The priesthood has always existed
- Joseph Smith History 1:68-74: Joseph Smith receives the priesthood
- Mosiah 18: Alma had authority to teach and baptize people
- Alma 13: Information on priesthood and responsibilities of priesthood holders
- Alma 17:3: The sons of Mosiah taught with authority and power
- 3 Nephi 11, 12, 18: Jesus Christ gives authority to the Nephites to baptize and give the Holy Ghost to others
- Doctrine and Covenants 20: Duties of Church members and priesthood holders
- Doctrine and Covenants 84: The Oath and Covenant of the Priesthood
- Doctrine and Covenants 107: Understanding the Aaronic and Melchizedek Priesthood
- Doctrine and Covenants 121: Vital lessons in how to use priesthood power and authority
- Doctrine and Covenants 132: Celestial marriage, the highest order of the priesthood

Exercising Priesthood Power and Authority in Righteousness

"Great women and men are always more anxious to serve than to have dominion."

—Spencer W. Kimball

There are times when both men and women can misuse their authority in church callings, at work, or even in their families. This is wrong! Priesthood keys, authority, or power should NEVER be used to manipulate, hurt, or force someone to do something.

In his time in Liberty Jail, Joseph Smith received a tremendous revelation about the best way to use priesthood power and authority. This revelation can be found in Doctrine and Covenants 121 and applies to both men and women. Verses 34-46 are critical in helping us understand the proper use of priesthood. In this revelation, the Lord tells why this revelation is needed: "We have learned by sad experience that it is the nature and disposition of almost all men, as soon as they get a little authority, as they suppose, they will immediately begin to exercise unrighteous dominion."

A mother who calls her children names and physically abuses them is exercising unrighteous dominion. A Young Men leader who creates contention in his quorum is practicing unrighteous dominion. A father who controls the family budget and does not counsel with his wife about it is using unrighteous dominion.

Why do people sometimes do this? In verse 37, the Lord tells us that selfishness, pride, vain ambition, and a desire for control often lie at the root of improper use of the priesthood. And the consequence is that "the heavens withdraw themselves" and "the Spirit of the Lord is grieved."

The Lord specifically outlines how we should use the priesthood in verses 41-45. The power should be used:
- With persuasion, long-suffering, gentleness, meekness
- With love unfeigned, kindness, with pure knowledge
- Without hypocrisy or guile

Sometimes we may need to reprove, or scold, someone when moved upon by the Holy Ghost. But then we need to show an increase of love toward that person afterward. The Lord also commands us to be full of charity and to do our best to keep the Holy Ghost as our constant companion. As we learn from these verses in Doctrine and Covenants 121, the powers of heaven cannot be used if someone is acting unkindly and unworthily. Priesthood is to be used for the benefit of others! We cannot use priesthood power or authority to unrighteously elevate ourselves.

"Self-mastery is essential to invoke the power of the priesthood of God. This is because this great, divine agency can only be exercised in righteousness."

—James E. Faust

Questions to Consider:

- What is unrighteous dominion?
- What is the proper way to use priesthood power and authority?
- What can you do if you think a church leader is abusing their priesthood authority?
- What can you do to make sure you are not abusing your priesthood responsibilities?

Priesthood power is amazing!

Don't wait until you are an adult to start learning about this special power you can access and use as soon as you have made your first covenants. Unlike worldly power that focuses on having power over others, priesthood power is all about caring for and loving others. We can use our spiritual gifts, the gift of the Holy Ghost, and this sacred power to be stronger, kinder, and to help others.

WHAT WILL YOU DO WITH YOUR PRIESTHOOD POWER?

Glossary

Aaronic Priesthood: The Aaronic Priesthood is not a different priesthood. It is the lesser portion of the priesthood. It is called the priesthood of Aaron because it was conferred on Aaron and his sons. It is an "appendage to . . . the Melchizedek Priesthood" (Doctrine and Covenants 107:14). It is sometimes called the preparatory priesthood because it prepares one for the higher priesthood. An Aaronic Priesthood holder administers in outward, preparatory ordinances, including baptism for the remission of sins.

Access: The right or ability to use, speak with, or enter.

Administer: To manage and carry out. The priesthood includes the authority to administer gospel ordinances, such as baptism and confirmation, that are necessary for salvation and exaltation.

Authority: The right someone has to make decisions, teach, and influence in their calling. This authority is given in the Church when someone is set apart by a leader with priesthood keys.

Confer: To bestow or grant upon another person.

Dispensation: A time period in which the Lord has at least one authorized servant on the earth who bears the holy priesthood and the keys.

Divine: Coming directly from God.

Endowment: A gift of spiritual knowledge and power for men and women to exercise priesthood power.

Levitical Priesthood: This order is a part of the Aaronic Priesthood. During the exodus from Egypt, the Levites were given priestly responsibilities concerning the tabernacle and always camped nearest to it. While the Levitical order does not function today, its privileges and authority are embraced within the Aaronic Priesthood for whatever future use the Lord may direct.

Melchizedek Priesthood: The higher or greater priesthood, as compared with the lesser or Aaronic Priesthood. The Melchizedek Priesthood is also called the priesthood "after the order of mine Only Begotten Son" (Doctrine and Covenants 124:123).

Oath and Covenant of the Priesthood: An oath is a sworn affirmation to be true and faithful to one's promises. A covenant is a solemn promise between two parties. The Oath and Covenant of the Priesthood is contained in Doctrine and Covenants 84.

Officiate: To be in charge of the priesthood ordinances done in one's jurisdiction.

Offices of the Priesthood: Apostle, bishop, deacon, teacher, priest, elder, high priest, seventy, patriarch, presiding high priest.

Ordination: When someone in authority appoints a worthy member to a new office in the priesthood.

Patriarchal Blessing: A special blessing where a person receives specific direction, warnings, and inspiration from God. In it, a person's lineage in the house of Israel is also given. In order to receive the blessing, a person must be interviewed by his or her bishop and then make an appointment with the stake patriarch.

Patriarchal Priesthood: Mentioned in the Doctrine and Covenants, this order is not a third, separate priesthood. The patriarchal order is a part of the Melchizedek Priesthood, which enables endowed and worthy men to preside over their posterity in time and eternity.

Priesthood Keys: The keys of the priesthood are the right to preside and direct the affairs of the Church within a jurisdiction. All priesthood keys are within The Church of Jesus Christ of Latter-day Saints, and no keys exist outside the Church on Earth.

Priesthood Power: A power available to all who receive priesthood ordinances and keep their covenants. This power enables a person to be strengthened and protected, receive personal revelation, and receive personal ministering by angels.

Preside: To be in charge or in a position of authority, such as a mother or father with their children.

Restoration: To return, restore, or renew something to its original state. Under the direction of Jesus Christ, Joseph Smith restored the fullness of the gospel to the earth.

Set Apart: A priesthood action where a person is formally blessed to carry out a specific calling or responsibility.

Works Cited:

"Aaronic Priesthood." The Church of Jesus Christ of Latter-day Saints, www.churchofjesuschrist.org/study/scriptures/bd/aaronic-priesthood?lang=eng.

Andersen, Neil L. "Preparing the World for the Second Coming." The Church of Jesus Christ of Latter-day Saints, Apr. 2011, www.churchofjesuschrist.org/study/general-conference/2011/04/preparing-the-world-for-the-second-coming?lang=eng.

Ballard, M. Russell. "Men and Women and Priesthood Power." The Church of Jesus Christ of Latter-day Saints, Sept. 2014, Ensign https://www.churchofjesuschrist.org/study/ensign/2014/09/men-and-women-and-priesthood-power?lang=eng.

Ballard, M. Russell. "'This Is My Work and Glory.'" The Church of Jesus Christ of Latter-day Saints, Apr. 2013, www.churchofjesuschrist.org/study/general-conference/2013/04/this-is-my-work-and-glory?lang=eng.

Beck, Julie B. BYU Women's Conference, Apr. 2011, womensconference.byu.edu/sites/womensconference.ce.byu.edu/files/julieb_openings.pdf.

Bingham, Jean B. "President Bingham on Women and Priesthood;The Lord Is Leading Us Gently Along." Church News, 12 May 2020, www.thechurchnews.com/leaders-and-ministry/2020-05-12/women-priesthood-covenant-president-bingham-lord-leading-revelation-181757.

Black, Susan Easton. *Glorious Truths about Mother Eve*. Covenant Communications, Inc., 2018.

Burton, Linda K. "Priesthood: 'A Sacred Trust to Be Used for the Benefit of Men, Women, and Children.'" BYU Women's Conference, 3 May 2013, womensconference.ce.byu.edu/sites/womensconference.ce.byu.edu/files/lindaburtontalk.pdf.

Burton, Linda K. "Priesthood Power-Available to All." The Church of Jesus Christ of Latter-day Saints, June 2014, www.churchofjesuschrist.org/study/ensign/2014/06/priesthood-power-available-to-all?lang=eng.

Cassler, Valerie Hudson. "I Am a Mormon Because I Am a Feminist." FairMormon, Sept. 2010, www.fairmormon.org/testimonies/scholars/valerie-hudson-cassler.

Caussé, Gérald. "Prepare the Way." The Church of Jesus Christ of Latter-day Saints, Apr. 2017, www.churchofjesuschrist.org/study/general-conference/2017/04/prepare-the-way?lang=eng.

Cordon, Bonnie H. "President Cordon on Women and Priesthood - Increased Power through Service." Church News, 19 May 2020, www.thechurchnews.com/leaders-and-ministry/2020-05-19/women-priesthood-covenant-president-cordon-power-service-kindness-spiritual-treasures-184179.

Dew, Sheri. "Sweet Above All That Is Sweet." BYU Women's Conference, May 2014, womensconference.byu.edu/sites/womensconference.ce.byu.edu/files/sheri_dew.pdf.

Dew, Sheri L. *Women and the Priesthood: What One Mormon Woman Believes*. Deseret Book, 2013.

Eyre, Aubrey. "Why Women in the Church Should Be Following President Nelson's Invitation to Study about the Priesthood." Church News, 5 Mar. 2020, www.thechurchnews.com/leaders-and-ministry/2020-03-05/lds-church-priesthood-women-president-nelsons-invitation-study-176292.

Eyring, Henry B. "Priesthood and Personal Prayer." The Church of Jesus Christ of Latter-day Saints, Apr. 2015, www.churchofjesuschrist.org/study/general-conference/2015/04/priesthood-and-personal-prayer?lang=eng.

Eyring, Henry B. "Walk with Me." The Church of Jesus Christ of Latter-day Saints, Apr. 2017, www.churchofjesuschrist.org/study/general-conference/2017/04/walk-with-me?lang=eng.

Eyring, Henry B. "Women and Gospel Learning in the Home." The Church of Jesus Christ of Latter-day Saints, Oct. 2018, www.churchofjesuschrist.org/study/general-conference/2018/10/women-and-gospel-learning-in-the-home?lang=eng.

Faust, James E. "The Power of Self-Mastery." The Church of Jesus Christ of Latter-day Saints, Apr. 2000, www.churchofjesuschrist.org/study/general-conference/2000/04/the-power-of-self-mastery?lang=eng.

Gardner, B. M. (2019, March). "Connecting Daughters of God with His Priesthood Power." Retrieved January 05, 2021, from https://www.churchofjesuschrist.org/study/ensign/2019/03/connecting-daughters-of-god-with-his-priesthood-power?lang=eng

Gardner, Barbara Morgan. "Helping Female Students Rise to Their Spiritual Privileges" Religious Studies Center, rsc.byu.edu/vol-18-no-3-2017/helping-female-students-rise-their-spiritual-privileges.

Gardner, Barbara Morgan. The Priesthood Power of Women: in the Temple, Church, and Family. Deseret Book, 2019.

Harkness, Lisa L. "Sister Harkness on Women and Priesthood - Blessings from Priesthood Covenants." Church News, 9 June 2020, www.thechurchnews.com/leaders-and-ministry/2020-06-09/women-priesthood-covenant-sister-harkness-blessings-covenants-183088.

Holmes, Douglas D. "What Every Aaronic Priesthood Holder Needs to Understand." The Church of Jesus Christ of Latter-day Saints, Apr. 2018, www.churchofjesuschrist.org/study/general-conference/2018/04/what-every-aaronic-priesthood-holder-needs-to-understand?lang=eng.

Jones, Joy D. "An Especially Noble Calling." The Church of Jesus Christ of Latter-day Saints, Apr. 2020, www.churchofjesuschrist.org/study/general-conference/2020/04/14jones?lang=eng.

Jones, Joy D. "President Jones on Women and Priesthood - Do You Feel Diminished?" Church News, 26 May 2020, www.thechurchnews.com/leaders-and-ministry/2020-05-26/women-priesthood-covenant-president-jones-authority-power-diminished-blessed-184168.

Kimball, Spencer W. "Our Sisters in the Church." The Church of Jesus Christ of Latter-day Saints, www.churchofjesuschrist.org/study/general-conference/1979/10/our-sisters-in-the-church?lang=eng.

Kimball, Spencer W. "Relief Society-Its Promise and Potential." Relief Society-Its Promise and Potential, https://www.churchofjesuschrist.org/study/ensign/1976/03/relief-society-its-promise-and-potential?lang=eng.

Kimball, Spencer W. "The Role of Righteous Women." The Church of Jesus Christ of Latter-day Saints, Oct. 1979, www.churchofjesuschrist.org/study/general-conference/1979/10/the-role-of-righteous-women?lang=eng.

MacKay, Michael Hubbard. Prophetic Authority: Democratic Hierarchy and the Mormon Priesthood. University of Illinois Press, 2020.

Maxwell, Neal A. "The Women of God." The Church of Jesus Christ of Latter-day Saints, www.churchofjesuschrist.org/study/general-conference/1978/04/the-women-of-god?lang=eng.

McConkie, Bruce R. "Our Sisters from the Beginning." The Church of Jesus Christ of Latter-day Saints, www.churchofjesuschrist.org/study/ensign/1979/01/our-sisters-from-the-beginning?lang=eng.

McConkie, Bruce R. "The Doctrine of the Priesthood." The Church of Jesus Christ of Latter-day Saints, www.churchofjesuschrist.org/study/general-conference/1982/04/the-doctrine-of-the-priesthood?lang=eng.

McConkie, Carolyn F. "Receive Heavenly Power in the Temple." Ensign College Main Site, 4 Feb. 2020, www.ensign.edu/devotionals/carolyn-f-mcconkie.

Millet, Robert L. "Restoring the Patriarchal Order." From an address given at the BYU Family Expo Conference in April 1998, Brigham Young University. Division of BYU Continuing Education.

Monson, Thomas S. "Do Your Duty." The Church of Jesus Christ of Latter Day Saints, Oct. 2005, www.churchofjesuschrist.org/study/general-conference/2005/10/do-your-duty-that-is-best?lang=eng.

Monson, Thomas S. "The Priesthood-a Sacred Gift." The Church of Jesus Christ of Latter-day Saints, Apr. 2015, www.churchofjesuschrist.org/study/general-conference/2015/04/the-priesthood-a-sacred-gift?lang=eng.

"Mother in Heaven." The Church of Jesus Christ of Latter-day Saints, Oct. 2015, www.churchofjesuschrist.org/study/manual/gospel-topics-essays/mother-in-heaven?lang=eng

"Nauvoo Relief Society Minute Book, Page 38." Joseph Smith Papers, www.josephsmithpapers.org/paper-summary/nauvoo-relief-society-minute-book/35.

Nelson, Russell M. "Spiritual Treasures." The Church of Jesus Christ of Latter-day Saints, Oct. 2019, www.churchofjesuschrist.org/study/general-conference/2019/10/36nelson?lang=eng.

Nelson, Russel M. "The Price of Priesthood Power." The Church of Jesus Christ of Latter-day Saints, Apr. 2016, www.churchofjesuschrist.org/study/general-conference/2016/04/the-price-of-priesthood-power?lang=eng.

Oaks, Dallin H. "Priesthood Authority in the Family and the Church." The Church of Jesus Christ of Latter-day Saints, Oct. 2005, www.churchofjesuschrist.org/study/general-conference/2005/10/priesthood-authority-in-the-family-and-the-church?lang=eng.

Oaks, Dallin H. "The Aaronic Priesthood and the Sacrament." The Church of Jesus Christ of Latter-day Saints, 1998, www.churchofjesuschrist.org/study/general-conference/1998/10/the-aaronic-priesthood-and-the-sacrament?lang=eng.

Oaks, Dallin H. "The Keys and Authority of the Priesthood." The Church of Jesus Christ of Latter-day Saints, Apr. 2014, www.churchofjesuschrist.org/study/general-conference/2014/04/the-keys-and-authority-of-the-priesthood?lang=eng.

Oaks, Dallin H. "The Powers of the Priesthood." The Church of Jesus Christ of Latter-day Saints, Apr. 2018, www.churchofjesuschrist.org/study/general-conference/2018/04/the-powers-of-the-priesthood?lang=eng.

Oscarson, Bonnie L. "Rise Up in Strength, Sisters in Zion." The Church of Jesus Christ of Latter-day Saints, Oct. 2016, www.churchofjesuschrist.org/study/general-conference/2016/10/rise-up-in-strength-sisters-in-zion?lang=eng.

Packer, Boyd K. "What Every Elder Should Know-and Every Sister as Well." The Church of Jesus Christ of Latter-day Saints, www.churchofjesuschrist.org/study/ensign/1993/02/what-every-elder-should-know-and-every-sister-as-well-a-primer-on-principles-of-priesthood-government?lang=eng.

Perry, Janice Knapp. "Love Is Spoken Here." The Church of Jesus Christ of Latter-day Saints, www.churchofjesuschrist.org/music/library/childrens-songbook/love-is-spoken-here?lang=eng.

Peterson, H. Burke. "Unrighteous Dominion." The Church of Jesus Christ of Latter-day Saints, www.churchofjesuschrist.org/study/ensign/1989/07/unrighteous-dominion?lang=eng.

"Priesthood." The Church of Jesus Christ of Latter-day Saints, www.churchofjesuschrist.org/study/manual/gospel-topics/priesthood?lang=eng.

"Priesthood Keys." The Church of Jesus Christ of Latter-day Saints, www.churchofjesuschrist.org/study/new-era/2012/05/priesthood-keys?lang=eng.

"Priesthood Principles." The Church of Jesus Christ of Latter-day Saints, www.churchofjesuschrist.org/study/manual/general-handbook/3-priesthood-principles?lang=eng.

Renlund, Dale, and Ruth Lybbert Renlund. *The Melchizedek Priesthood*. Deseret Book, 2018.

Smith, Joseph Fielding. "Magnifying Our Callings in the Priesthood." The Improvement Era, June 1970, https://archive.org/details/improvementera7306unse/page/n67.

Snow, Erastus. "There Is a God, Etc." Journal of Discourses, jod.mrm.org/19/266.

Stevenson, Gary E. "Sacred Homes, Sacred Temples." The Church of Jesus Christ of Latter-day Saints, Apr. 2009, www.churchofjesuschrist.org/study/general-conference/2009/04/sacred-homes-sacred-temples?lang=eng.

Talmage, James E. *The House of the Lord*. Church of Jesus Christ of Latter-day Saints, 1979.

"Teachings of Presidents of the Church: Joseph Smith." The Church of Jesus Christ of Latter-day Saints, www.churchofjesuschrist.org/bc/content/shared/content/english/pdf/language-materials/36481_eng.pdf?lang=eng.

Uchtdorf, Dieter F. "Be Not Afraid, Only Believe." The Church of Jesus Christ of Latter-day Saints, Nov. 2015, www.churchofjesuschrist.org/study/liahona/2015/11/general-priesthood-session/be-not-afraid-only-believe?lang=eng.

Uchtdorf, Dieter F. "The Greatest among You." The Church of Jesus Christ of Latter-day Saints, Apr. 2017, www.churchofjesuschrist.org/study/general-conference/2017/04/the-greatest-among-you?lang=eng.

Uchtdorf, Dieter F. "Your Potential, Your Privilege." The Church of Jesus Christ of Latter-day Saints, Apr. 2011, www.churchofjesuschrist.org/study/general-conference/2011/04/your-potential-your-privilege?lang=eng.

Ulrich, Wendy. *Live up to Our Privileges: Women, Power, and Priesthood*. Deseret Book, 2019.

"Women and the Priesthood." The Church of Jesus Christ of Latter-day Saints, www.churchofjesuschrist.org/study/manual/the-latter-day-saint-woman-basic-manual-for-women-part-a/women-in-the-church/lesson-13-women-and-the-priesthood?lang=eng.

Note from the Author:

I enjoy studying about priesthood power, but my interest really began when I was a teenager growing up in Glendale, California. I was especially intrigued when I received the following counsel in my patriarchal blessing: "I bless you to enjoy the spirits which will be entrusted to the care of you and your husband; to love them and preside over your family with your husband as equal partners, each with some special responsibilities . . ."

Even as a teenager I knew this was how priesthood should function in a home, but this wasn't always confirmed in Sunday School or youth meetings. Like many other members of The Church of Jesus Christ of Latter-day Saints, I have wondered, pondered, and prayed for a greater understanding regarding priesthood power. I have also heard and read many truths that have led me to further prayer and personal revelation on the topic. **What I've learned has shown me children need to be taught much earlier of their divine potential and of their priesthood power and responsibilities!**

I'm so grateful to Heavenly Parents who have entrusted us, such imperfect beings, with this incredible power that we might serve and lift our fellow brothers and sisters on the earth.

If you would like further information and inspiration into priesthood power, authority, and keys, I recommend the books *Women and the Priesthood* by Sheri Dew, *The Priesthood Power of Women* by Barbara Morgan Gardner, and *The Melchizedek Priesthood* by Dale and Ruth Renlund. Each of these books, as well as scriptures and talks from general authorities, provide wonderful insight and understanding of this complex topic.

**IF YOU ENJOYED THIS BOOK,
PLEASE LEAVE A POSITIVE REVIEW ON AMAZON.COM**

You may also enjoy these books available on Amazon.

Record Your Impressions

Record Your Impressions

Made in the USA
Middletown, DE
01 June 2024